GIANTS OF THE OLD TESTAMENT

LESSONS ON LIVING FROM
JOSHUA

A devotional by

WOODROW KROLL

BACK TO THE BIBLE ®

JOSHUA
published by Back to the Bible
©1998 by Woodrow Kroll

International Standard Book Number
0-8474-0684-9

Edited by Rachel Derowitsch
Cover concept by Robert Greuter
& Associates

For information:
BACK TO THE BIBLE
POST OFFICE BOX 82808
LINCOLN, NEBRASKA 68501

1 2 3 4 5 6 7 8—04 03 02 01 00 99 98

Printed in the USA

CONTENTS

DAY 1

Exodus 24:12-13

*Then the L*ORD *said to Moses, "Come up to Me on the mountain and be there; and I will give you tablets of stone, and the law and commandments which I have written, that you may teach them." So Moses arose with his assistant Joshua, and Moses went up to the mountain of God.*

Clap and Cheer

Little Jamie Scott was trying out for a part in his school play. His mother knew he had his heart set on being in the play, but she feared he wouldn't be chosen. On the day the parts were awarded, apprehensively she picked him up after school. To her surprise, Jamie came rushing out, his eyes shining with pride and excitement. "Guess what, Mom!" he shouted. "I have a part! I've been chosen to clap and cheer."

God calls some of us to be in the limelight; others He calls to "clap and cheer." At this point in his life, Joshua was asked to do the latter. It would be 40 years before he became the leader of Israel. In the meantime, he was a supporter and assistant to Moses. And he did it well. Whether it was battling with the Amalekites (Ex. 17:10) or providing moral support as Moses met with the Lord on

Mount Sinai, Joshua served the Lord by being an encouragement to the His servant.

Those whom God calls to serve Him in leadership face many challenges. Often they carry deep responsibilities and heavy spiritual burdens. At times they are the target of malicious gossip or hurtful behavior. You can understand how important it is that they have around them some mature believers who are there to "clap and cheer" for them. What a blessing such encouragement can be!

Have you given any thought to how you might be an encouragement to the servants of God whom you know? Who encourages your pastor or his wife? Who cheers on the Sunday school teacher or the workers at the homeless shelter? What can you do today to lighten their load and lift their spirits? So many are prone to criticize and complain. Perhaps God has a part for you. Commit yourself to "clap and cheer" and you'll be the hit of the play.

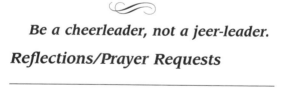

Be a cheerleader, not a jeer-leader.

Reflections/Prayer Requests

DAY 2

Exodus 32:17-18

And when Joshua heard the noise of the people as they shouted, he said to Moses, "There is a noise of war in the camp." But [Moses] said: "It is not the voice of those who shout in victory, nor is it the voice of those who cry out in defeat, but the voice of those who sing that I hear."

Deceived by the Noise

Lost in the jungle, a man sought desperately to find his way to safety. His strength was ebbing fast. Suddenly he heard what he thought was a bell tolling in the distance. Surely civilization must be near by. Valiantly he struggled on, but never seemed to draw closer to the sound. Finally he fell to the ground exhausted, never to rise again. The uncanny call of the South American bellbird, which sounds like a reverberating "toll," had struck again. Instead of offering the weary traveler promised safety, it lured him to his death.

Joshua made a similar mistake. When he heard the sounds of shouting, his military mind immediately assumed he was hearing the sounds of battle. But Moses, experienced in the ways of human nature, realized it was something even more sinister. What Joshua mistook for the sounds of potential physical danger, Moses recognized as the sure sounds of serious moral danger. Instead of war, it was the noise of debauchery and immorality.

Satan is a skilled noisemaker, and he loves to disguise the reality of sin with deceitful noise. He cloaks his wicked ways with words that sound lofty and noble. He hides his lies and deceit beneath raucous laughter, emotional appeals or apparent sincerity. The consequences, however, are spiritual disaster or even death.

Don't be fooled by the noise. Always take what you hear back to the Word of God. If it's not consistent with the Bible, take no heed to it no matter how good it sounds.

Check out the words you hear by the Word you trust.

Reflections/Prayer Requests

_____

_____

_____

_____

_____

_____

_____

_____

DAY 3

Numbers 11:27-29

And a young man ran and told Moses, and said, "Eldad and Medad are prophesying in the camp." So Joshua the son of Nun, Moses' assistant, one of his choice men, answered and said, "Moses my lord, forbid them!" Then Moses said to him, "Are you zealous for my sake? Oh, that all the LORD's people were prophets and that the LORD would put His Spirit upon them!"

Zealous for What?

How easy it is to misplace our zeal. Around 1420 A.D., "golfe" or "the Gouf" became so popular that King James II of Scotland feared the pastime placed the country at risk in its ongoing war with England. He reasoned that his men were spending too much time chasing the "golfe" ball and too little time practicing archery. Consequently the king persuaded his government to pass an act of parliament banning "golfe." Obviously, his zeal was misplaced, not to mention ineffective.

Joshua also had a misplaced zeal. As the assistant to Moses, he considered it his responsibility to make sure his master's power and influence were not threatened. Since part of Moses' authority stemmed from the fact that God spoke through him, the thought of others prophesying or speaking for the Lord disturbed

Joshua. In his enthusiasm to protect his master's position, he was ready to hinder the proclamation of God's Word.

Over the centuries, God has used many instruments to proclaim His Word. Sometimes these instruments possessed questionable motives. The apostle Paul noted that some "preach Christ from selfish ambition, not sincerely" (Phil. 1:16). His conclusion? "What then? Only that in every way, whether in pretense or in truth, Christ is preached; and in this I rejoice, yes, and will rejoice" (v. 18).

Our zeal must primarily focus on the message, not the messenger. If the Word of God is being faithfully proclaimed, let's rejoice. God sometimes chooses the least likely to speak for Him. If someone is not a true spokesman for Him, God will take care of that. We need not worry.

Be zealous for the message; God will judge the messenger.

Reflections/Prayer Requests

_____

_____

_____

_____

_____

_____

DAY 4

Numbers 13:1-2, 16

*And the L<small>ORD</small> spoke to Moses, saying,
"Send men to spy out the land of Canaan,
which I am giving to the children of Israel;
from each tribe of their fathers you shall send
a man, every one a leader among them.*

*These are the names of the men whom
Moses sent to spy out the land. And Moses
called Hoshea the son of Nun, Joshua.*

Fulfilling Our Responsibilities

The British naval hero Lord Nelson took his responsibilities very seriously. During his life he conscientiously served his nation in its ongoing conflict with France and Spain. Fatally wounded in the battle at Trafalgar, Nelson said before he died, "Thank God, I have done my duty."

Joshua carried heavy responsibilities as well. He was a leader among the people of his tribe. He was one of 12 chosen to spy out the land of Canaan. Later he would become Moses' right-hand man in leading the armies of Israel against their enemies. In fact, Moses gave him the nickname "Joshua," which means "he shall save his people." That was a tremendous responsibility to live up to as well. Yet with God's help, Joshua was able to come to the end of his days with the confidence that he had successfully fulfilled all the duties God had given him.

Most of us discover early that life has many obligations. There is schooling to complete, a family to raise, a job to perform, a church to support, bills to be paid, and so much more. And, if God calls you into leadership, there are usually additional commitments that come with your position. Some days can seem a bit overwhelming.

But don't be overpowered by it all. With God's help, you also can complete your responsibilities. When you get swamped, take time out, get alone with God in some secluded place, and read His Word for encouragement and strength. Ask God's Spirit to refresh you and to provide the wisdom you need to successfully fulfill all that is set before you. Be faithful to your obligations and discover the satisfaction of a life well lived.

Being responsible before God is being responsive to God.

Reflections/Prayer Requests

DAY 5

Numbers 14:28-30

"Say to them, 'As I live,' says the LORD, 'just as you have spoken in My hearing, so I will do to you: the carcasses of you who have murmured against Me shall fall in this wilderness, all of you who were numbered, according to your entire number, from twenty years old and above. Except for Caleb the son of Jephunneh and Joshua the son of Nun, you shall by no means enter the land which I swore I would make you dwell in.'"

Faithfulness Rewarded

It was a stormy night in Birmingham, England, and Hudson Taylor was to speak at a meeting at the Severn Street schoolroom. His hostess assured him that nobody would attend on such a stormy night, but Taylor insisted on going. "I must go even if there is no one but the doorkeeper." Fewer than a dozen people showed up, but the meeting was marked with unusual spiritual power. Half of those present either became missionaries or gave their children as missionaries; and the rest were faithful supporters of the China Inland Mission for years to come. Taylor was faithful and God rewarded him.

Faithfulness always has it rewards, both in heaven and on earth. Joshua stood faithful to God's promises. When the ten spies brought back discouraging reports about the land of Canaan, Joshua and his partner, Caleb, stood firm on God's assurance of victory. When the people threatened to stone him, he refused to back down from his convictions. It's no wonder, therefore, that Joshua and Caleb were given the privilege of entering the Promised Land when everyone else was condemned to die in the wilderness.

Being faithful often puts you on the wrong side of popular opinion. Standing steadfast on the Word of God can make you the object of ridicule, if not hatred. Being firm about your beliefs sometimes causes people to think of you as narrowminded, unenlightened or even worse. But be faithful to what you know is right. Ultimately your faithfulness will be rewarded.

Don't be discouraged by what others say or do. Be faithful to God's Word and His work. God promises He will make it all worthwhile.

Faithfulness is the process; God's blessings are the product.

Reflections/Prayer Requests

_____

_____

_____

_____

DAY 6

Numbers 32:11-12

*Surely none of the men who came up
from Egypt, from twenty years old and above,
shall see the land of which I swore
to Abraham, Isaac, and Jacob, because they
have not wholly followed Me, except Caleb
the son of Jephunneh, the Kenizzite,
and Joshua the son of Nun, for they have
wholly followed the L*ORD*.*

Total Commitment

A few years ago, prominent members of society gathered in the Saints Peter and Paul Church in San Francisco for a wedding. The bride was dazzling in her wedding gown and the service was elegant in its execution. But when it came to that all-important moment to say "I do," the bride hesitated and then replied, "I just can't make up my mind." The minister waited a moment and then announced to the audience that the wedding was off. The reception was canceled and thousands of dollars' worth of food was given away. A week later, however, the bride asked for the wedding to proceed. Her uncertainty, she claimed, "was just do to nerves."

Fortunately, Joshua, along with Caleb, never had such moments of uncertainty. No less than five times (Num. 32:12; Deut. 1:36; Josh. 14:8, 9, 14) the Bible says Joshua "wholly" followed the Lord. There was no hesitation, no second thoughts, no vain regrets. Instead, he gave himself to be and do all that God desired of him. His life had no room for a "maybe," or a tentative "let me think about it." Joshua's mind was made up; he would totally serve the Lord.

When it comes time to give a clear testimony for the Lord, Christians often seem to be afflicted with a bad case of the nerves. They stutter and stumble and just can't seem to "make up their minds." George Gallup, in his studies on American church life, noted that America is a nation of nominal believers, many belonging to a church but few attending. They just can't make up their minds to take a stand for the Lord.

Let's put behind us all our indecisiveness. When the opportunity comes to take a stand for Christ, whether by witnessing for Him or simply identifying with a local assembly of believers, don't hesitate. "Wholly" follow the Lord.

A holy response comes from a wholly committed heart.

Reflections/Prayer Requests

_____

_____

_____

_____

DAY 7

Deuteronomy 1:37-38

The LORD was also angry with me [Moses] for your sakes, saying, "Even you shall not go in there; but Joshua the son of Nun, who stands before you, he shall go in there. Encourage him, for he shall cause Israel to inherit it."

The Value of Encouragement

Francois Arago, a 19th-century French astronomer, attributed his success to words he found written on the paper cover of his book at a time when he was greatly discouraged. These words, written by French mathematician and philosopher Jean d'Alembert, were, "Go on, sir; go on! The difficulties you meet will resolve themselves as you advance. Proceed, and light will dawn and shine with increased clearness on your path." Following these simple words made Arago the first astronomical mathematician of his age.

God knew that Joshua would need encouraging words as well. Moses had become so discouraged with the grumbling people that he himself sinned against the Lord and lost his opportunity to enter the Promised Land (Num. 20:8-20). Therefore, God instructed Moses to challenge all the people to encourage his young understudy. If Joshua were to fulfill his mission, the monumental task of leading Israel into the land of Canaan, the people needed to support him with their encouragement.

You and I are much the same. We need encouragement, too, whether we're a leader or a follower. George M. Adams observed that "encouragement is oxygen to the soul." If we plan to go on living, we need oxygen; if we plan to go on serving the Lord, we need encouragement.

Do you have the gift of encouragement? Whom can you comfort today? What simple word can you say that will go a long way in motivating your friends or family? Make it your ministry to lift the spirits of those around you so that they can serve the Lord more effectively.

If you want to be encouraged, encourage someone else.

Reflections/Prayer Requests

_____

_____

_____

_____

_____

_____

_____

DAY 8

Wisdom From Above

Life is filled with predicaments that require wisdom. Two men were hiking when they spotted a mountain lion staring at them. One froze in his tracks, but the other sat down on a log, tore off his hiking boots, pulled a pair of running shoes from his backpack and hurriedly began to put them on. "For crying out loud, you can't outrun a mountain lion!" his companion said. "I don't have to," the other shrugged. "I just have to outrun you."

There is some wisdom to what this man said, but this type of earthly wisdom is not sufficient to accomplish God's purposes. Joshua needed much more than common sense if he were to be the leader God wanted him to be. Therefore, as Moses laid hands upon him in prayer, God granted Joshua a supernatural measure of wisdom through His Holy Spirit.

God still offers such wisdom today. James says, "If any of you lacks wisdom, let him ask of God, who gives to all liberally and without reproach, and it will be given to him" (James 1:5). But this is not just any wisdom; it is a godly wisdom. James calls it "the wisdom that is from above" (3:17). God, who is the giver of all good gifts, delights in giving godly wisdom to those who truly desire it. We all need it; do we all desire it as well?

If you are facing a situation that calls for real wisdom, don't settle for earthly wisdom. So much more is available to you. Ask God to give you the wisdom that comes from above. Only by godly wisdom can you meet God's expectations.

Godly work always requires godly wisdom.

Reflections/Prayer Requests

_____

_____

_____

_____

_____

_____

_____

_____

_____

_____

DAY 9

Joshua 1:5

"No man shall be able to stand before you all the days of your life; as I was with Moses, so I will be with you. I will not leave you nor forsake you."

Never Forsaken

In 1970 an Arizona lawyer named Russel T. Tansie filed a $100,000 damage suit against God. The suit was filed on behalf of Mr. Tansie's secretary, Betty Penrose, who accused God of negligence in His power over the weather when He allowed a lightning bolt to strike her home. The woman won the case when the Defendant failed to appear in court. I wonder if she ever collected?

When trials come or disaster strikes, it's easy to feel as if God is being negligent. When something we can't explain happens, we believe God has let us down. But the Bible makes it very clear that this is not true. God told Joshua that He would not leave nor forsake him. Actually, in the Hebrew language, the negative comes first and makes the thought even stronger: "not will I leave you" and "not will I forsake you." The order of these words emphasizes the fact that, no matter how difficult Joshua's circumstances might become, God would not leave and He would not forsake. He was as committed to Joshua as He had been to Moses. Could you use that same kind of commitment from God today? You have it. Read Hebrews 13:5.

God's presence doesn't mean that things will always go smoothly. Christians don't walk around with protective plastic bubbles surrounding them. We experience cancer; we endure sorrow and heartache; we fail in business. God's promise, however, is that He will continue to walk with us and be faithful to us even in our sorrows or failures. His company will bring you comfort that will exceed your understanding (Phil. 4:7).

Be assured that as God was with Moses and Joshua, He is with you as well. Jesus promised, "I am with you always, even to the end of the age" (Matt. 28:20). Whatever difficulties you face, you will not have to face them alone. He will never, no never, fail you nor forsake you. That's His promise to you.

Only God can say never—and really mean it.

Reflections/Prayer Requests

_____

_____

_____

_____

_____

DAY 10

Joshua 1:8

This Book of the Law shall not depart from your mouth, but you shall meditate in it day and night, that you may observe to do according to all that is written in it. For then you will make your way prosperous, and then you will have good success.

The Key to Good Success

My local newspaper reported that a man and woman who tried to hop a Union Pacific train from North Platte, Nebraska, to Omaha were being held in Dawson County jail on trespass charges. But the couple wouldn't have gotten to Omaha even if they hadn't been apprehended; the train was headed to Kansas City.

Many people who think they're on the train headed for success are really going in the opposite direction. History is awash with examples of men and women who found a form of success, but lived to regret it. It was not what the Bible calls "good" success. Lord Byron, who achieved fame both as a poet and a libertine, wrote at the age of 35:

My days are in the yellow leaf,
The flowers and fruits of love are gone;
The worm, the canker, and the grief
Are mine alone.

God's success is far different; it's always headed in the right direction. Joshua was assured that if he lived consistent with what was written in God's Word, he would achieve success—but not just any success. God's promise to Joshua, as well as to you and me, is that if we live by all that is written in the Bible, we will achieve "good" success.

The key to good success is obedience to God's Word. If you conform your life to God's will, as it is revealed in His Word, you'll experience the kind of success that will be a blessing rather than a burden.

Only a good God can give good success.

Reflections/Prayer Requests

_____

_____

_____

_____

_____

_____

_____

_____

_____

DAY 11

Joshua 1:9

Have I not commanded you? Be strong and of good courage; do not be afraid, nor be dismayed, for the Lord your God is with you wherever you go.

Strong and Courageous

A child had to walk each evening past a dark, spooky house. Some adult friends tried to give him courage. One handed him a good-luck charm to ward off the ghosts. Another installed a light at a particularly dark corner near the house. A third took a more spiritual approach, saying, "It's sinful to be afraid. Trust God and be brave!" It was good advice, but not much help. Then one friend said with compassion, "I know what it is to be afraid. I'll walk with you past the house." Instantly the child's fears were gone.

This was what God did for Joshua. Joshua faced the fearful task of leading a group of nomads against the trained armies of established kingdoms. That was enough to make even the bravest man tremble. But God did more than give Joshua a battle plan or a pep talk; He reassured him, saying, "I will be with you wherever you go."

God does not promise He will not lead you into fearful situations. He may call you to serve Him in a land far from your friends and family. For most of us this challenge could be frightening. Or God may ask you to stand against the tide of popular opinion on your school board or at a city council meeting. And again your knees may knock and your voice tremble. But just like Joshua, you can do it because God also has given you the solution for your fears: He has given you Himself.

In Christ you have strength for every weakness and the courage for every fear. The psalmist said, "Yea, though I walk through the valley of the shadow of death [literally, the valley of dark shadows], I will fear no evil; for You are with me; Your rod and Your staff, they comfort me" (Ps. 23:4). Are you facing a formidable task? Trust God's presence to dispel your fears and give you renewed strength and courage.

Courage is spelled C-H-R-I-S-T.

Reflections/Prayer Requests

_____

_____

_____

_____

_____

_____

_____

DAY 12

Joshua 1:12-14

And to the Reubenites, the Gadites, and half the tribe of Manasseh Joshua spoke, saying, "Remember the word which Moses the servant of the LORD commanded you, saying, 'The LORD your God is giving you rest and is giving you this land.' Your wives, your little ones, and your livestock shall remain in the land which Moses gave you on this side of the Jordan. But you shall pass before your brethren armed, all your mighty men of valor, and help them."

Promise Keepers

In his book *Up From Slavery*, Booker T. Washington described meeting an ex-slave from Virginia: "The man had made a contract with his master, two or three years previous to the Emancipation Proclamation, that permitted him to buy his freedom. While he was paying for himself, his master released him to labor where and for whom he pleased. Finding he could receive better wages in Ohio, he journeyed there. When Abraham Lincoln declared all slaves to be free, however, the man was still in debt to his master three hundred dollars. Even though technically he was freed from any obligation, he still walked back to where his old master lived in Virginia and placed the last dollar, with interest, in his hands. The man concluded,

'I could not enjoy my freedom until I had fulfilled my promise.'"

Joshua, too, reminded the Reubenites, the Gadites and half the tribe of Manasseh that they had made a promise during the days of Moses. In return for being allowed to settle in the peaceful land east of the Jordan, they agreed to join their kinsmen in conquering the land west of the river. It was now time to fulfill that promise.

God expects all of us to keep our promises. In fact, the psalmist said that the person who walks with integrity "swears to his own hurt, and does not change" (Ps. 15:4).

Is there a promise that you need to fulfill? Have you made a commitment and not seen it to the end? Now is the time to take your obligation seriously and make good on your promises. Even if technically you're off the hook, people of integrity always do what they promise.

A promise broken is a responsibility left undone.

Reflections/Prayer Requests

_____

_____

_____

_____

_____

DAY 13

Joshua 3:1

Then Joshua rose early in the morning; and they set out from Acacia Grove and came to the Jordan, he and all the children of Israel, and lodged there before they crossed over.

Early in the Morning

During the American Revolution, it is reported that Colonel Rahl, commander of the British troops at Trenton, New Jersey, was playing cards when a courier brought an urgent message stating that General George Washington was crossing the Delaware River. Rahl put the letter in his pocket and didn't bother to read it until the game finished. Then, realizing the seriousness of the situation, he hurriedly tried to rally his men to meet the coming attack. It was too late. His procrastination was his undoing. He and many of his men were killed, and the rest of the regiment was captured.

Unlike Colonel Rahl, Joshua was one commander who didn't hesitate to take action. The job ahead was a major one: lead the people of Israel across the flooded Jordan and into Canaan. Roaring downward toward the Dead Sea, the current of the Jordan is very swift at Jericho. In addition, the melting snows in the Lebanon mountains caused the river to overflow at this season of the year. The task must have been intimidating. You could understand if Joshua chose to stall as long as possible. But instead of procrastinating, he "rose early in the morning" and began to rally the people for the trip ahead of them.

When faced with tasks that are frightening or disagreeable, many people choose to put them off as long as possible. They find excuses to avoid unpleasant situations or make difficult decisions. But what a mistake that is. Often it only makes matters worse.

If you are faced with a challenging situation, don't procrastinate. Trust in God's strength and wisdom. Claim His promises of presence and protection. Then, get up "early in the morning" and go to it. At the end of the day, you'll be glad you did.

A job never started is a job never finished.

Reflections/Prayer Requests

_____

_____

_____

_____

_____

_____

DAY 14

Joshua 3:7

And the LORD said to Joshua, "This day I will begin to magnify you in the sight of all Israel, that they may know that, as I was with Moses, so I will be with you."

Exalted by God

How quickly man-made greatness fades! Before he attacked Russia, Napoleon Bonaparte seemed to have the world at his feet. But the Russian invasion turned into a disaster and Napoleon, fearing his position at home was in danger, left the French army and hurried back to France almost unaccompanied. Arriving at a river crossing, Napoleon inquired of the ferryman whether many deserters had come that way. Not recognizing the famous leader, the man responded, "No, you are the first."

God does not deal in such fleeting fame. What He offered to Joshua was something far better than anything man could give. As Joshua responded in obedience to God's Word, the Lord assured him that He would exalt him. Just as God had brought honor to Moses, so would He bring honor and respect to Joshua. This would not be a human grab for glory, but a gracious gift from God.

God offers the same to every Christian. As we make Christ the center of our lives and His Word the focal point of all that we say or do, the Lord will bring to us a glory that will outlast any honor that man could bestow. While we may not always be recognized by the movers and shakers of this world, the Scriptures assure us that we will be revealed in all our glory when Christ returns (1 Pet.1:7).

Don't worry if those around you fail to praise you. Seek instead for the honor that comes from the Lord. That glory will last forever.

Eternal greatness can come only from an eternal God.

Reflections/Prayer Requests

_____

_____

_____

_____

_____

_____

_____

_____

_____

DAY 15

Joshua 3:13

"And it shall come to pass, as soon as the soles of the feet of the priests who bear the ark of the LORD, the Lord of all the earth, shall rest in the waters of the Jordan, that the waters of the Jordan shall be cut off, the waters that come down from upstream, and they shall stand as a heap."

Wet Feet

Years ago visitors at one of the national mints were told by a guide that if they first dipped their hands in water, a ladle of molten metal could be poured over their outstretched palms without burning them. A husband and wife were part of this group. "Perhaps you would like to try it," the guide said to the husband. The husband drew back sharply, "No thanks," he said. "I'll take your word for it." The mint employee turned to the wife. "Would you like to try it?" She replied, "Certainly." She pulled up the sleeve of her blouse and thrust her hand into a bucket of water. Calmly she held her hand out while the metal was poured over it. It's obvious that the husband believed at one level, but he wasn't willing to put his belief to the test. The wife believed on a completely different level. She was willing to take a risk.

Joshua and his people also were faced with a risk. They needed to cross the dangerous, flood-swollen Jordan. God had previously opened the Red Sea when the people had to cross it, but this time the priests had to step into the water first and trust the Lord to open the way as they went. They had to get their feet wet and trust that God would honor their faith.

Many Christians dislike taking risks. They want the way opened before they move out for God. Often He graciously honors their desire. But we must remember that a risk is only a risk if God doesn't go with you. We need to step out and trust that God will confirm our faith at the appropriate time.

If your way seems blocked today, step forward by faith. Be willing to get your feet wet and then wait for God to respond.

God honors wet feet, not cold feet.

Reflections/Prayer Requests

_____

_____

_____

_____

_____

_____

_____

_____

DAY 16

Joshua 4:1-3

*And it came to pass, when all the people had completely crossed over the Jordan, that the L*ORD *spoke to Joshua, saying: "Take for yourselves twelve men from the people, one man from every tribe, and command them, saying, 'Take for yourselves twelve stones from here, out of the midst of the Jordan, from the place where the priests' feet stood firm. You shall carry them over with you and leave them in the lodging place where you lodge tonight.'"*

A Family Memorial

The memory capacity of an ordinary human mind is astonishing. You may not consider yourself particularly good at remembering technical data, but think about how many faces you can recognize or how many names you can recall. Consider also how you are able to remember some past incident or how many words you can spell and define. Someone has estimated that in a lifetime, a brain can store one million billion "bits" of information. Yet how easy it is to forget the marvelous things that God does for us.

For that reason God commanded Joshua to select 12 men, one from each tribe, to pick up a stone from the dry riverbed and carry it to where they would lodge. These 12 stones became a reminder to the people of the miracle that the Lord performed for them. But this memorial was not for them alone. Joshua instructed the people, "When your children ask their fathers in time to come, saying, 'What are these stones?' then you shall let your children know, saying, 'Israel crossed over this Jordan on dry land'" (4:21-22). These stones became a family memorial.

It's important for every family to have reminders of what the Lord has done for them. Perhaps you could keep a journal of God's blessings in your life. A friend of mine has a photo album that helps her and her family remember the Lord's goodness.

However you choose to do it, just do it. Begin today to build a family memorial to the Lord. Your grandchildren and great-grandchildren will thank you.

A family that remembers the Lord will be blessed forever.

Reflections/Prayer Requests

_____

_____

_____

_____

_____

DAY 17

Joshua 5:9

Then the LORD said to Joshua, "This day I have rolled away the reproach of Egypt from you." Therefore the name of the place is called Gilgal to this day.

Rolled Away

According to one source, Americans spend $50 million a year on subliminal message tapes designed to help them do everything from improve their self-image to learn a foreign language. Unfortunately, the National Research Council has concluded that subliminal messages simply don't work. Despite all the hype to the contrary, these tapes don't deliver the life-transforming changes they promise.

But there is one source who always delivers on His promises—God. As the Israelites prepared to enter the Promised Land, they needed to renew their covenant with God. This relationship required that circumcision be performed as a sign of the covenant. Those Israelites who left Egypt had been circumcised, but those males born during the wilderness wandering had not (vv. 4-5). It was now time for the younger generation to take their stand and have the "reproach of Egypt" rolled away.

Circumcision is no longer a sign of the covenant relationship with God. When Jesus died on the cross, the outward sign of circumcision was replaced with the inner presence of the Holy Spirit. He is the fulfillment of the promise in Ezekiel: "I will give you a new heart and put a new spirit within you; I will take the heart of stone out of your flesh and give you a heart of flesh" (Ezek. 36:26). When the Holy Spirit comes in, the old life is rolled away and we become "a new creation" in Christ (2 Cor. 5:17).

This experience can be yours as well. If you are still walking in your old life, why not receive Christ today and let Him roll your sins away? The reproach of the past can be replaced with a hope for the future.

Christ doesn't improve you; He transforms you.

Reflections/Prayer Requests

_____

_____

_____

_____

_____

_____

_____

DAY 18

Joshua 5:13-15

And it came to pass, when Joshua was by Jericho, that he lifted his eyes and looked, and behold, a Man stood opposite him with His sword drawn in His hand. And Joshua went to Him and said to Him, "Are You for us or for our adversaries?" So He said, "No, but as Commander of the army of the LORD I have now come." And Joshua fell on his face to the earth and worshiped, and said to Him, "What does my Lord say to His servant?"

The "What Man"

While watching his father tune up the family car, a five-year-old boy announced, "I know what I want to be when I grow up. I want to be a 'what man'!" His puzzled father asked him to explain, so the little boy elaborated, "A 'what man' has a place where people bring their cars when there is something wrong with them, and he tells them what to do."

Israel had reached a point in their invasion plans where they also needed a "what man." Jericho was surrounded by fortified walls and defended by trained soldiers. Both were seemingly insurmountable obstacles. Yet as Joshua stood near the city, pondering what to do, the Commander of the Lord's army appeared to him. Most Bible scholars believe this to be a pre-incarnate appearance of Christ.

Joshua fell down before Him and said, "Tell me what you want me to do."

Often in life we need a "what man." Situations arise leaving us totally confused about what to do. That's when we need to turn to the Lord. Only the Lord God is capable of being our "what man." He has a plan for us that works out all the "whats" and "whys" of life. Through Jeremiah the prophet, He said, "For I know the thoughts that I think toward you, says the Lord, thoughts of peace and not of evil, to give you a future and a hope" (Jer. 29:11).

Seek the Lord, read His Word daily, and find out what His will is for you. Avail yourself of His wisdom and you'll discover that He always knows what to do.

The "what" is never a secret to God.

Reflections/Prayer Requests

_____

_____

_____

_____

_____

_____

_____

_____

_____

DAY 19

Joshua 6:3-5

"You shall march around the city, all you men of war; you shall go all around the city once. This you shall do six days. . . . But the seventh day you shall march around the city seven times, and the priests shall blow the trumpets. Then it shall come to pass, when they make a long blast with the ram's horn, and when you hear the sound of the trumpet, that all the people shall shout with a great shout; then the wall of the city will fall down flat."

It's a Mystery to Me

In speaking of things beyond our understanding, the famous orator and statesman William Jennings Bryan declared, "I have observed the power of the watermelon seed. It has the power of drawing from the ground and through itself 200,000 times its weight. When you can tell me how it takes this material and out of it colors an outside surface beyond the imitation of art, and then forms inside of it a white rind and within that again a red heart, thickly inlaid with black seeds . . . when you can explain to me the mystery of a watermelon, you can ask me to explain the mystery of God."

Joshua was faced with the mystery of God as well. Upon hearing the plan given by God, surely someone must have asked him, "How will marching around a wall, blowing trumpets and shouting knock down that wall?" Certainly it was beyond understanding. But the mysteries of God usually are.

Divine mysteries abound. We don't understand how a child could be conceived without a father, but it happened (Luke 1:34). We can't comprehend how an infinite God could be housed in a finite human body, but He was (Col. 1:15). It's beyond our comprehension that one man's death could pay for the sins of the world, but it did (Rom. 5:18). We don't understand, but that's okay. God's mysteries are not for us to explain; they are for us to accept by faith and act upon.

If you're struggling to understand a mystery of God, don't trouble yourself. The real issue is not whether you understand; it's whether you are willing to obey.

Faith obeys when explanations are lacking.

Reflections/Prayer Requests

_____

_____

_____

_____

_____

_____

DAY 20

Joshua 7:3-5

And they returned to Joshua and said to him, "Do not let all the people go up, but let about two or three thousand men go up and attack Ai. Do not weary all the people there, for the people of Ai are few." So about three thousand men went up there from the people, but they fled before the men of Ai. And the men of Ai struck down about thirty-six men, for they chased them from before the gate as far as Shebarim, and struck them down on the descent; therefore the hearts of the people melted and became like water.

Let the Victor Beware

On November 16, 1776, Fort Washington fell to the advancing British troops and General Washington was forced to retreat. Secure in his victory, General Howe chose not to pursue the Continental army, but ordered his men into winter quarters instead. On Christmas night, Washington ferried a portion of his troops back across the Delaware and mounted a surprise attack. The British were caught off guard and more than a thousand Hessian soldiers were taken prisoner. On the heels of victory, the British experienced a stinging defeat.

Joshua had the same experience. After an overwhelming victory at Jericho, his soldiers were routed by the defenders of a pile of rubble (Ai literally means "ruin"). While the defeat was brought about by sin in the camp (7:10-13), the attitude of those in leadership was one of arrogance and conceit. Their overconfidence set them up for a humiliating defeat.

Someone has said that the most vulnerable moment for a Christian is the moment following a spiritual victory. We are often basking in the glow of our accomplishments. Our guard is down. And Satan knows that this is a prime time to attack.

If you are experiencing a time of spiritual success, give God the glory. At the same time, be on guard. Continue with your spiritual disciplines and maintain an attitude of watchfulness. As the Scriptures warn, "Let him who thinks he stands take heed lest he fall" (1 Cor. 10:12).

The more "puffed up" you are, the better target you make.

Reflections/Prayer Requests

_____

_____

_____

_____

_____

_____

DAY 21

Joshua 7:11-12

*"Israel has sinned, and they have also trans-
gressed My covenant which I commanded
them. For they have even taken some
of the accursed things, and have both stolen
and deceived; and they have also put it
among their own stuff. Therefore the children
of Israel could not stand before their enemies,
but turned their backs before their enemies,
because they have become doomed
to destruction. Neither will I be with you any-
more, unless you destroy the accursed
from among you."*

It Only Hurts Me

We never sin alone. A study of 8,415
adults revealed that those exposed to sec-
ondhand smoke experienced a 10 percent
increase in the thickening of their carotid
arteries, which supply blood to the brain.
Thickening of the carotid arteries is a
major cause of strokes. Other statistics
indicate that drug and alcohol abuse is
costing businesses more than $60 billion a
year in absenteeism, workplace accidents,
higher insurance costs, waste and low
productivity. This cost is passed on to con-
sumers in the prices of goods and ser-
vices.

Achan may have thought that his sin
affected only him. Yet when Joshua went
before the Lord to find out why his army

had been defeated at Ai, God said, "Israel sinned." Achan's sin caused grief to Joshua (vv. 6-7), to the families of the 36 men struck down at Ai (v. 5) and especially to his own family (vv. 24-25). Achan's sin not only hurt him, but everyone around him.

People still excuse their sin by saying, "It doesn't hurt anyone but me." But the facts prove otherwise. Sin hurts everybody either directly or indirectly. A study claimed that a New York City subway token, which costs $1.25, would cost only $1.19 if no one evaded fares. The cost of a property-casualty policy costs $600, but if no one committed fraud, it would be $540. A spreadsheet software package costs $495, but if no one pirated programs, it would only be $322.

The next time Satan encourages you to sin, just remember that you won't be the only one who gets hurt. Sin hurts all of us.

Satan is the only one who comes out ahead when we sin.

Reflections/Prayer Requests

DAY 22

Joshua 8:1

Then the LORD said to Joshua: "Do not be afraid, nor be dismayed; take all the people of war with you, and arise, go up to Ai. See, I have given into your hand the king of Ai, his people, his city, and his land."

Solid As the Rock

Gibraltar is a small peninsula of the southern coast of Spain near the entrance to the Mediterranean Sea. Covering most of this peninsula is an enormous mass of limestone 1,398 feet high. This rocky mass has become a symbol of stability and certainty, and from which we get our expression, "Solid as the Rock of Gibraltar."

Yet God's word is just as solid—and even more so. Three times God spoke to Joshua of future events that were as good as done. In chapter 6, God said of Jericho, "See! I have given Jericho into your hand, its king and the might men of valor" (v. 2). And that's what happened. In chapter 8, He said to Joshua concerning Ai, "See, I have given into your hand the king of Ai, his people, his city, and his land" (v. 1). Sure enough, it came about (vv. 18-25). Then in chapter 10, God promised Joshua victory over the Amorites, saying, "Do not fear them, for I have delivered them into your hand" (v. 8). Again, God came through on His word (vv. 10-11).

While the Rock of Gibraltar will some day crumble, God's words never will. Jesus promised, "Heaven and earth will pass away, but My words will by no means pass away" (Matt. 24:35). In a day of instability and change, we can be confident that what God says, He will do. What He declares, He will perform.

If you are feeling bewildered by upheaval in your life, look to the Rock—not the rock of Gibraltar, but the Rock of Jesus. Take Him at His word; He will never change.

Don't settle for the rock when you can have the Rock.

Reflections/Prayer Requests

_____

_____

_____

_____

_____

_____

_____

_____

_____

_____

DAY 23

Joshua 9:3-6

But when the inhabitants of Gibeon heard what Joshua had done to Jericho and Ai, they worked craftily, and went and pretended to be ambassadors. And they took old sacks on their donkeys, old wineskins torn and mended, old and patched sandals on their feet, and old garments on themselves; and all the bread of their provision was dry and moldy. And they went to Joshua, to the camp at Gilgal, and said to him and to the men of Israel, "We have come from a far country; now therefore, make a covenant with us."

Making Godly Decisions

Decisions are part of our life every day. We decide what to wear when we get up in the morning. We decide what to eat, what to listen to on the radio or watch on television. We make a multitude of other less-than-earthshaking choices daily. But sometimes we face decisions that have a major impact on our lives. These may affect whom we marry, where we live or what job we hold. But big or small, the choices we make should honor the Lord.

Joshua was faced with an important decision soon after he entered the land of Canaan. God had warned him not to make treaties with any of the neighboring peoples. Yet when a group of people showed up who claimed to live far away, he had to reject or accept their plea for peace. Carefully Joshua and his advisors inspected the moldy food and worn-out clothing. Yet verse 14 says, "but they did not ask counsel of the Lord." Only after they had finalized the agreement did they learn they had been tricked.

Deception and misrepresentations are rampant in our society. Salespeople try to rush us into making immediate decisions. Television promotes an unrealistic view of life. Advertisers imply promises they can't fulfill. In the midst of it all, we need to seek the counsel of the Lord. Only the principles in His Word will enable us to make choices that consistently honor Him.

When you need to make a decision, don't rely on human wisdom alone, but look to God's Word. Ask Him to reveal His truths that will enable you to make wise and godly decisions.

When the right decision is important, the right counsel is imperative.

Reflections/Prayer Requests

_____

_____

_____

_____

DAY 24

Joshua 10:12-13

Then Joshua spoke to the LORD in the day when the LORD delivered up the Amorites before the children of Israel, and he said in the sight of Israel: "Sun, stand still over Gibeon; and Moon, in the Valley of Aijalon." So the sun stood still, and the moon stopped, till the people had revenge upon their enemies. Is this not written in the Book of Jasher? So the sun stood still in the midst of heaven, and did not hasten to go down for about a whole day.

The Power of Bent Knees

Have you ever wondered how a bird can sleep on its perch and never fall off? The secret is the tendons of the bird's legs. They are constructed in such a way that when the leg is bent at the knee, the claws contract and grip like a steel trap. The claws refuse to let go until the knees are unbent again.

It was the bent knee that gave Joshua his power as well. As the Israelites were pursuing their enemy the Amorites, they were running out of daylight. It was a critical time because, even though the battle had been won, the route was not complete. In the sight of all Israel, Joshua stopped and called upon the Lord, and the sun stood still in the midst of the sky. Joshua 10:14 declares, "And there has been no day like that, before it or after it, that the LORD heeded the voice of a man; for the LORD fought for Israel." That's the power of the bent knee!

If you want power with God, you need to practice bending your knees. While every prayer will not stop the sun, every prayer that reflects God's will can win your battle. Prayer is God's chosen instrument to release His power in our daily life.

Determine today to practice the power of prayer. Set aside a daily time to bend the knee and seek the Lord. Discover for yourself the life-changing effects that can be brought about through bent knees.

When you need to hang on tight, bend your knees.

Reflections/Prayer Requests

_____

_____

_____

_____

_____

_____

_____

_____

_____

_____

DAY 25

Joshua 14:6-7

Then the children of Judah came to Joshua in Gilgal. And Caleb the son of Jephunneh the Kenizzite said to him: "You know the word which the LORD said to Moses the man of God concerning you and me in Kadesh Barnea. I was forty years old when Moses the servant of the LORD sent me from Kadesh Barnea to spy out the land, and I brought back word to him as it was in my heart."

Friends in Deed

Dr. Abraham Maslow, famed research analyst, estimated that the average American meets only about 50 percent of his need for love, interpersonal support and intimacy. In the latter stages of his research, Dr. Maslow became even more negative in his summary: "The truth is," he said, "the average American does not have a real friend in the world."

That stands in stark contrast to the friendship we see between Joshua and Caleb. First teamed up by Moses as partners to explore the land of Canaan, they also stood steadfast together when the people rebelled and wanted to stone them (Num. 14:6-10). Joshua was later selected to replace Moses as the leader of Israel, but that seemed to have no effect on their friendship. Forty-five years later we find them fighting shoulder to shoulder as

Israel sought to solidify its hold on the Promised Land. And in the midst of the conflict, Joshua fulfilled a promise. Joshua 14:13 says, "And Joshua blessed him, and gave Hebron to Caleb the son of Jephunneh as an inheritance."

Joshua and Caleb were friends indeed and friends in deed. It was a friendship tested by time and trials, but a friendship expressed in commitment and deeds. What had been promised in words was fulfilled in deeds.

Perhaps you are blessed with such a friend as Caleb. If so, find a way today not only to say how much you appreciate this friend but to show it as well. Follow the admonition of 1 John 3:18: "Let us not love in word or in tongue, but in deed and in truth."

A friend in deed is a friend indeed.

Reflections/Prayer Requests

_____

_____

_____

_____

_____

_____

_____

DAY 26

Joshua 18:2-3

But there remained among the children of Israel seven tribes which had not yet received their inheritance. Then Joshua said to the children of Israel: "How long will you neglect to go and possess the land which the LORD God of your fathers has given you?"

How Long?

Some people refuse to wait. On June 22, 1997, Thomas and Corilee McClurkin peacefully celebrated their golden anniversary. But it wasn't that way 50 years ago. The month of June in 1947 was exceptionally soggy in Nebraska. The Loup River flooded it banks and stranded the bride-to-be in her hometown of Poole. Undaunted, Thomas set out in knee-deep water in an old Chevy. Upon reaching a flimsy railroad bridge that had been nearly washed away, he abandoned his car, crawled across the bridge and walked to Ravenna. Once there he persuaded the owner of a two-seat airplane to fly him to Poole to pick up his bride. The marriage took place only 13 hours late.

This kind of eagerness, however, seemed to be lacking among the Israelites. Seven of the tribes had yet to make any headway in possessing their inheritance. Even though God promised that He would give them the land, they failed to move forward aggressively. Joshua's accusation (v. 3) implies that the problem was not with availability but with motivation. How long, he wondered, were they going to wait?

The same question could be asked of many Christians. How long will it be before we avail ourselves of the vast spiritual riches God has made possible? He has given us the privilege of life-changing prayer. He has made it possible for us to study His Word in any number of translations. We are new creatures in Christ, with all the potential that can be found in such a position. When will we possess these riches?

Don't delay. Begin today to possess all the spiritual benefits God offers you. Now is the time for you to take what God has promised.

God can only give what you are willing to take.

Reflections/Prayer Requests

_____

_____

_____

_____

_____

DAY 27

Joshua 22:4

And now the LORD your God has given rest to your brethren, as He promised them; now therefore, return and go to your tents and to the land of your possession, which Moses the servant of the LORD gave you on the other side of the Jordan.

Rest for the Weary

William Booth, the founder of the Salvation Army, received a letter from his wife while he was on a long trip. She wrote in part, "Your Tuesday's notes arrived safe, and I was rejoiced to hear of the continued prosperity of the work, though sorry you were so worn out. I fear the effect of all this excitement and exertion upon your health, and though I would not hinder your usefulness, I would caution you against an injudicious prodigality of your strength. Remember a long life of steady, consistent, holy labor will produce twice as much fruit as one shortened and destroyed by spasmodic and extravagant exertions; be careful and sparing of your strength when and where exertion is unnecessary."

God also is aware of this truth. After five years of battles, Joshua declared, "God has given rest." It was not that the land had been completely conquered, but it was time for the people to rest anyway.

Some Christians are quick to remind us that "Satan never takes a vacation." That may be true, but Satan is not the example we want to follow. One scholar who studied the Gospels claims that during the three years of Jesus' ministry, ten periods of resting are mentioned. If Jesus felt it necessary to punctuate His ministry with seasons of rest, how much more so should we.

Being alone and resting for a while is not selfish; it's Christlike. Taking a vacation is not fleshly; it's spiritual. God's kingdom is not advanced by those who work themselves into a coronary or nervous breakdown. God gives rest to the weary, so don't be too proud to take it.

Come apart for rest or you may come apart forever.

Reflections/Prayer Requests

_____

_____

_____

_____

_____

_____

_____

_____

_____

DAY 28

Joshua 23:6-8

Therefore be very courageous to keep and to do all that is written in the Book of the Law of Moses, lest you turn aside from it to the right hand or to the left, and lest you go among these nations, these who remain among you. You shall not make mention of the name of their gods, nor cause anyone to swear by them; you shall not serve them nor bow down to them, but you shall hold fast to the LORD your God, as you have done to this day.

Pass It Along

Sometimes we wonder why God allows certain things to happen to us. "Why did God allow my child to die?" "Why was I stricken with cancer?" "Why do I have to face such a struggle with finances?" There's no one answer that fits every situation. But sometimes God allows us to undergo certain experiences so we can pass along the things we learn to those following us.

As he assumed the leadership of Israel, Joshua faced times of great fear and uncertainty. In the midst of those difficulties, God encouraged him with the exhortation, "only be strong and very courageous" (1:7). Furthermore, the Lord commanded him, "This Book of the Law shall not depart from your mouth . . . that you may observe to do according to all that is written in it" (1:8). Joshua had learned a great deal from the hardships he suffered and, as he approached the latter years of his life, he shared this wisdom with the ones who would be leaders after he was gone.

As God's people, we have a responsibility to pass on to the younger generation those truths God has taught us. Some call this "mentoring." The apostle Paul exhorted both Timothy and Titus to encourage the older generation to be teachers and encouragers of those who are younger (2 Tim. 2:2; Titus 2:3-5).

Don't waste the wisdom God has shared with you. Sometimes younger people don't seem to want to listen, so be creative in your mentoring. Learn to pass on truth in the form of stories or even write them in a notebook. Don't let the truths God has taught you go to waste.

If God considers it a lesson worth learning, we must consider it worth sharing.

Reflections/Prayer Requests

_____

_____

_____

_____

_____

DAY 29

Joshua 24:13

"I [God] have given you a land for which you did not labor, and cities which you did not build, and you dwell in them; you eat of the vineyards and olive groves which you did not plant."

Not for Sale

During the Spanish-American War, Clara Barton, the founder of the Red Cross, was working in Cuba. One day Colonel Theodore Roosevelt came to her and offered to buy food for some of his sick and wounded Rough Riders. But she refused to sell him what he wanted. Roosevelt could not understand. He cared about his men, and he was willing to pay for the supplies out of his own funds. So he went to the surgeon in charge, who said to him, "Colonel, just ask for it!" A smile broke over Roosevelt's face. Now he understood—the provisions were not for sale. "I will ask for it," he said, and when he did, he got the food at once.

Joshua reminded the people that all they possessed—their land, their cities and their vineyards—were not the result of their own efforts. Certainly they had confronted the enemy. Obviously they had engaged in many dangerous and bloody battles. But those victories were not the ultimate source of their possessions. Instead, all that they owned was a gift from God.

God is not in the retail business. All of our good deeds, our generous gifts, our religious activities could not begin to buy our salvation. But God is willing to give it to us. When we receive Christ as our Savior, all that God has is ours for the asking.

Enjoy God's gracious gifts today. Thank Him for providing them without price and without cost. They are yours not because you buy them, but because God gives them.

God's gifts are free, but they are not cheap.

Reflections/Prayer Requests

_____

_____

_____

_____

_____

_____

_____

_____

_____

_____

DAY 30

Joshua 24:15

*"And if it seems evil to you to serve
the L<small>ORD</small>, choose for yourselves this day
whom you will serve, whether the gods
which your fathers served that were on the
other side of the River, or the gods of the
Amorites, in whose land you dwell. But as for
me and my house, we will serve the L<small>ORD</small>."*

You've Got to Choose

Sometime ago many newspapers carried a story about a woman who was divorcing her husband after discovering he had two other wives and several children by each of them. His explanation? He couldn't bear the thought of hurting any of them, so he had married all three. He was a traveling salesman, so he was able to carry out the farce for several years. Rather than facing a hard choice, he took the easy way out.

Once established in the Promised Land, the Israelites also were confronted with a multitude of choices. And the choices weren't necessarily easy. They could worship the gods of Egypt. These were gods that their parents had known from their long years of servitude. Familiarity made that tempting. On the other hand, the gods of the Amorites, the nation they had conquered, offered opportunities to indulge the flesh, which many likely found attractive.

Some may have stood betwixt and between, but Joshua was not afraid to make the hard decision. Boldly he declared, "As for me and my family, we will serve the Lord."

Choosing to serve the Lord is not always an easy decision. Sometimes it means going against the religious beliefs of your family. Other times peer pressure and the desire to "fit in" make us hesitant to declare openly our commitment to the Lord. Many people find it easiest to behave like a chameleon, changing colors to fit whatever group they happen to be with. But that only temporarily avoids making the hard decision.

Today, decide to take a stand. Whom will you serve? Will it be yourself? Will it be the gods of pleasure or wealth or ease? Or will you choose the God who loves you? Making a decision for Christ may be hard, but it's a choice you will never regret.

The easy choice is seldom the right choice.

Reflections/Prayer Requests

_____

_____

_____

_____

_____

DAY 31

Judges 2:6-8

And when Joshua had dismissed the people, the children of Israel went each to his own inheritance to possess the land. So the people served the LORD all the days of Joshua, and all the days of the elders who outlived Joshua, who had seen all the great works of the LORD which He had done for Israel. Now Joshua the son of Nun, the servant of the LORD, died when he was one hundred and ten years old.

A Lasting Influence

A soap advertisement depicted a little fellow looking intently at his shadow, which fell across his pathway. The slogan underneath the picture read, "That's the only thing I can't wash out!" This clever bit of sales promotion is also a good reminder of the indelible shadow of influence we cast on others by our example.

The Bible records that Joshua not only had a long life, but he had an influential life as well. The way Joshua chose to live influenced the people of his generation and also the "elders who outlived Joshua." His example made a lasting impact on the younger generation that took the leadership role after him. While eventually the nation of Israel fell away from the Lord, that was delayed by Joshua's godly influence for at least another generation.

Wrong attitudes and actions can engrave an impression on young minds that is impossible to erase. But just as we can leave a permanent mark for evil, we also can leave a lasting effect for good. We should strive to live so that our loving spirit, vibrant faith and purity of life are never diluted by inconsistency.

Consider that what you choose to do will continue on long after you are gone. Live in such a way that when you stand before the Judgment Seat of Christ, you will not be ashamed of your influence.

Let your light so shine that it will cast the right kind of shadow.

Reflections/Prayer Requests

_____

_____

_____

_____

_____

_____

_____

_____

_____

_____